FROM ANGELS' HOLY HANDS

JENNIFER HOPPEL

From Angels' Holy Hands
by Jennifer Hoppel
Copyright © 2025 Jennifer Hoppel

ISBN 978-1-63360-311-0

All rights reserved. This book is protected under the copyright laws of the United States of America. This book may not be copied or reprinted for commercial gain or profit.

Scriptures marked NIV are taken from THE HOLY BIBLE: New International Version ©1978 by the New York International Bible Society, used by permission of Zondervan Bible Publishers. All rights reserved.

Scriptures marked NLT are taken from the Holy Bible, New Living Translation, copyright © 1996, 2004, 2015 by Tyndale House Foundation. Used by permission of Tyndale House Publishers, Inc., Carol Stream, Illinois 60188. All rights reserved.

Scriptures marked NKJV are taken from the New King James Version®. Copyright ©1982 by Thomas Nelson. Used by permission. All rights reserved.

oFor Worldwide Distribution
Printed in the U.S.A.

Urban Press
P.O. Box 8881
Pittsburgh, PA 15221-0881
412.646.2780

Contents

Foreword	v
Fruitful Suffering	vii
Introduction	xv

Chapter 1
As I Am — 1

Chapter 2
Smile in the Rain — 19

Chapter 3
The Homegoing Service — 32

Chapter 4
Ranger Boback — 43

Chapter 5
Mars — 53

Chapter 6
Teen Idolatry — 63

Chapter 7
Hansel and Gretel — 75

Chapter 8
Blessed Are Those Who Mourn — 87

Chapter 9
They Survived — 101

Chapter 10
The Father's Love — 108

Afterword — 113

My Brother, My Friend,

This is my brother Robert James Alexander Hoppel, my best friend in the world. On August 4, 1985 he entered this life to change it forever, to change us forever. He lived with a passion and energy and intensity that surpassed us all. He was a born leader, a character builder. He was straightforward and [brutally] honest. He was gentle and compassionate to all God's creatures (especially cats). He would never hurt anyone or thing on purpose. He was created to worship. He loved music and people more than anything else. He had a special way of making us love him back. He always made an impact. Nothing in the world hurt him more than to see people divided. He hated walls and barriers. He understood what was really important and as a result invested his life in each one of us.

His life was filled with everything he loved. He played with the DC Youth Orchestra, Montgomery County Youth Orchestra, Georgetown Symphony, Whitman bands, Oakbrook and New Covenant worship teams. His lifelong dream of having his own band came true just this past year with the youth band. Violin, percussion, guitar, singing, composing –he was so gifted. Through all his activities he made lifelong friends and filled people's lives with joy and laughter. He traveled to Austria and Wales. He had his dream job working at Jammin' Java. When I picked him up after his interview, his smile was huge! He talked for hours about the studio and concerts and how to correctly make espresso. His enthusiasm could have easily out-promoted their PR department.

But what was best about Robert was how he mirrored the image of Christ. So much of Jesus showed through him. He was open and honest about his strengths and weaknesses. He was real and sincere about everything. He was one of the few people who did his best to live God's definition of love (See 1 Cor. 13). And Robert, as I sit here - struggling with how to say goodbye - I thank you the most for pointing your life towards our Brother and Friend, Jesus Christ. I'm going to miss you so much. I love you. Until we meet again ...

Your sister,

Rebekah

Foreword

Fruitful Suffering

On June 7, 2023, a day which would have been my father's 110th birthday (he died in 1991 at the age of 77 from lung cancer), I was seeking the Lord for what to say in the Introduction of a book I am getting ready to publish, *From Angels' Holy Hands*. It had been twenty-two years since the tragic death of our son, and while it had been my intention for quite some time to write a book, I never seemed able to get past the Introduction.

How do you introduce a book about suicide? How do you introduce a book about the suicide death of a fifteen-year-old child? It seemed to me that the Introduction should carry some answers, some advice, some words of wisdom and hope that would help others who find themselves in circumstances similar to the ones that surrounded the life and death of our precious son.

But in twenty-two years, I had found

none—no answers, no advice, no words of wisdom to pass on to onlookers who, along with all of us who knew and loved my son so well, were asking why? Why does a handsome, well-liked, talented young boy spend a day playing with his friends, swimming in a lake, laughing, loving, teasing, and caring, and then suddenly run off into the woods to hang himself? How could this have happened? What could he possibly have been thinking? Where did we fail him?

Upon seeking the Lord's guidance on how to begin, I sensed Him speaking to my heart: "I chose you and appointed you that you should go and bear fruit and that your fruit should remain ... that whatever you ask the Father in My Name, He may give you. These things I command you that you love one another" (John 15:16-17, NKJV).

Another Scripture was speaking to my heart at the same time: "Go, for he is a chosen vessel of Mine to bear My name before Gentiles, kings, and the children of Israel. For I will show him how many things he must suffer for My names' sake" (Acts 9:15-16, NKJV). These are unusual Scriptures when searching for guidance on how to write the Introduction to a book about suicide. But then something clicked. I sensed the Lord say to me that He chose and appointed me for a purpose and the purpose has something to do with suffering, just like Saul was chosen and appointed for a purpose—and part of that purpose included suffering. I had never before seen the connection between God choosing us, appointing us, sending us, and suffering for His name's sake.

I had walked with the Lord for nearly ten years and had never encountered any suffering. I was saved at the age of 18 through a Bible verse in the bulletin of a Methodist Church I was attending at the time: "for the Son of Man has come to seek and to save that which was lost" (Luke 10:10, NKJV). Then I was baptized in the Holy Spirit shortly thereafter. Life had its ups and downs and there were certainly challenges I had to overcome, but nothing that I would put into a category of suffering.

I can remember the day I gave birth to our first child, our daughter, Rebekah Kara, and I thought that was suffering. In fact, I was in so much pain that I had the silliest of notions that I was coming close to the pain that Jesus must have felt while on the cross. While thinking of Jesus' suffering on the cross did help me overcome the pains of childbirth, the suffering a woman endures during labor and delivery doesn't come close to the suffering Jesus was alluding to in Acts 9:16 concerning Saul or the suffering He Himself endured on the cross.

And then there's this Scripture where Jesus had just finished telling his disciples to give a message to John the Baptist who was in prison, "… blessed is he who is not offended because of Me" (Matthew 11:6, NKJV). Why did Jesus say this? Did He anticipate John the Baptist being offended because he was in prison and Jesus wasn't coming to get him out? Did Jesus anticipate the disciples being offended because He wasn't going to drop everything and use His miraculous powers to spring His cousin out of jail? He certainly could have but He didn't. And why?

There's that question again that has kept me from being able to write the book about the suicide death of my fifteen-year-old son. Why didn't God heal him? Why didn't He stop him from taking his own life? He certainly could have. I have plenty of reasons for which I could be offended with Jesus and God. But seen in the context of suffering, all this makes perfect sense. John the Baptist, the disciples, and the Apostle Paul suffered much during their lifetimes on earth with Jesus. If they weren't exempt from suffering, what makes us think that we should be?

In July of 1988 I was traveling with my five-year-old daughter and three-year-old son to a music teacher's house for violin lessons. My father was a worship leader in his generation, having studied at Julliard, and was an accomplished musician and worship director in multiple churches, playing the organ, directing choirs. He was excited to see his grandchildren starting musical training of their own. I was passionate about worship myself and looking to start the kids' music lessons while they were young so that they could have every opportunity to be the best they could be for the Lord and His service.

My daughter, Rebekah, was in the front seat of the car (legal in that day), and my son, Robert, in a booster seat in the back. I was 27 weeks pregnant with our not-yet-born son, David. A woman ran a red light, striking my car as I was making a left-hand turn with the green arrow light in our favor. We were all injured in the car accident, including my child in utero who suffered a stroke that resulted in a hypoxic brain injury, causing innumerable, immeasurable consequences for our young and fledgling family of five.

Our son, David, fought for his life the remaining ten weeks of my pregnancy as it was discovered at birth when he had a blood sugar level of zero that my placenta had been destroyed and he had been getting no nutrients from the time of the car accident until birth. All of us suffered, including my husband who had to close down a business that he had spent a lifetime dreaming about to get a job that carried better health insurance. David required intense medical and educational care for many years as the doctors who at first gave us little hope that he would survive, but when he did, then gave us no guarantee that he would ever walk or talk.

One doctor offered us a glimmer of hope. The geneticist from Children's National Medical Center told us that the complications resulting from the stroke in utero could be rehabilitated much as the complications resulting from an adult stroke victim can be, but we would have to work very, very hard to try to get the side of the brain that was not injured to take over some of the functions of the side of the brain that was.

I could have been offended at God for all of this – the car accident, the financial stress, the medical and educational challenges that lay before us. I could have blamed God for this, but I didn't. We needed His help, and help us He did. We have multiple testimonies of God's provision – His saving grace – beginning with the testimony of a secret service agent who witnessed the car accident and was able to testify in court that it was indeed the lady who ran the red light when she tried to blame the accident on me!

David not only learned to walk and talk but went on to earn a master's of divinity and is currently a hospice chaplain living in Florida. David's birth and life is a miracle and a testament to the Resurrection power of the Coming One, the message Jesus sent the disciples back to John the Baptist with "the blind see and the lame walk; the lepers are cleansed and the deaf hear; the dead are raised up and the poor have the gospel preached to them" (Matthew 11:5, NKJV). Our son, David, 36 as I write, is a living testimony to this Word.

But there is still the question why.

God did it for David; why didn't He do it for Robert? Was this something we were appointed to? Suffering through no fault of our own? Have we been appointed to overcoming unthinkable odds in life and death–clinging to our confidence that we truly **can** do **all** things through Christ who strengthens us? Can the lessons we have learned along the way be the fruit that Jesus wants us to bear in the midst of it all?

I'm still not sure how many answers I have, but I want to share my journey and some answers in the pages that follow. This book took me a long time to write but I am finally confident that our story, even if we don't have a lot of answers, will serve to encourage and sustain you in your own times of asking the simple question, Why?

Introduction

I read many books on the topic of grieving after our teenage son, Robert, died. Some ministered to my spirit and others didn't. A book that ministered the most was by Gregory Floyd, *A Grief Unveiled*. Mr. Floyd lost his six-year-old son who was killed in the front yard of his house by a friend who had lost control of his car. The author's writings have a fragrance of forgiveness permeating each and every page and, while he doesn't hide the devastating emotions of the grieving process he went through, it is clear to the reader that he was not bitter and had forgiven his friend. He truly understood and embraced the way of the cross, "Father, forgive them, for they know not what they do."

This is a significant mountain which Christians must face in times of great trials. We must scale the heights and depths of bitterness, unforgiveness, anger, and hatred that stand between us and healing and comfort.

These mountains prevent us from reaching the rivers of waters of the living Christ that the Lord promises will flow from the hearts of those who are thirsty and heavy laden. God is serious when He tells us to pray – "Forgive us our trespasses as we forgive those who trespass against us."

The body of our son, Robert James Alexander Hoppel, was found hanging from a tree after an all-day search by family, friends, volunteers, and state park rangers with helicopters and blood hounds on Sunday, May 28, 2001. He did not die at the hands of another. His own hands took his life – hands that used to connect with the God he loved in worship; hands that in an irreversible moment of time succumbed to the pressure of a mind that told him that life on earth was not worth living.

Many people, both noble and ignoble, understand this kind of pressure – Job, Jonah, and King David in the Bible to name a few. Robert was a child, still learning and growing. He had written a chorus to a song he was working on *From Angels' Holy Hands* but hadn't been able to put any verses to the song:

From Angels' Holy Hands
By Rob James A. Hoppel

I don't know exactly how
So I thought I would ask
How you came to me that night
With love's gold light
Cross my fingers at my back
And I'll pray for your return
From Angels' Holy Hands
From Angels' Holy Hands

I was really excited when I heard it – I told him that the words reminded me of a child in the womb – never making it to life to see his or her destiny fulfilled for whatever reason: abortion, premature birth, miscarriage. It reminded me of the kindness of God and what it would be like for that child – never taking a breath on earth but carried up to heaven nonetheless for a life with God in eternity: "from Angels' Holy Hands." I sensed the words were unspoken words from the spirit of a child witnessing the light that so many people speak of when passage to eternity is near. I asked Robert to consider these thoughts and he just looked at me, with that look he always used to give me when my thoughts didn't line up with his and said in that infamous tone, "Mom …"

My brother wrote in an op-ed article in the *Greensboro News and Record* on July 2001:

> This tragic end to an intense and all too short life was the result of an impulsive act. Had Robert had two minutes to reflect on what he had done, I am sure that he would have said, "Whoops! I shouldn't have done that!" But he didn't have those two minutes. Suicide is not a video game. It is real. It lasts forever. For those of us who are left behind, his friends and his family, we have to face the fact that he chose to cut off our relationship – permanently – without our permission. That results in anguish, some denial, some anger, and the need to do something.

I needed to write this book. I needed to document the struggle our son endured. He was a prolific writer of songs and journal entries that document well the struggle of his young, productive, yet turbulent life.

His time of "delivery" had not yet come. It is to his life and the deposit he left with us that this book is dedicated. And to the God he loved and served, a God we trust – a merciful God, who we believe sympathizes with all weakness, including the weakness of suicide, and delivered our frail, broken son, most tenderly from earth to heaven, "From Angels' Holy Hands."

I wouldn't be human if I told you that my heart was not broken. My heart has been shattered. But it is not bitter. The suicide death of my 15-year-old son has not separated me from the love of God. God is bigger than the circumstances of life. And His Heart is able to hold us in our grief. We serve a God who sympathizes with our weaknesses and who, in all things, was tempted, yet without sin. He is always there. Nothing can separate us from His love. Not even suicide.

> Through the LORD's mercies we are not consumed,
> Because His compassions fail not.
> They are new every morning;
> Great is Your faithfulness.
> "The LORD is my portion," says my soul,
> "Therefore I hope in Him!"

> The Lord is good to those who wait for Him,
> To the soul who seeks Him.
> It is good that one should hope and wait quietly
> For the salvation of the Lord.
> It is good for a man to bear
> The yoke in his youth.
>
> Let him sit alone and keep silent,
> Because God has laid it on him;
> Let him put his mouth in the dust—
> There may yet be hope.
> Let him give his cheek to the one who strikes him,
> And be full of reproach.
>
> For the Lord will not cast off forever.
> Though He causes grief,
> Yet He will show compassion
> According to the multitude of His mercies.
>
> – Lamentations 3:22-32

Jennifer Hoppel
Cabin John, Maryland
July 2025

CHAPTER 1
AS I AM

Monday: May 28, 2001

Dear Steve, Jenny, Rebekah, David and Joshua:

Word has just come of Robert's tragic and untimely death. We are weeping and aching with you. There are no words adequate to express the depth of our feelings for you at this time, knowing that you are going through inexpressible pain. Only God and His Word can sustain you right now.

Paul said in 1 Thessalonians 4:13-18,

And now, brothers and sisters, I want you to know what will happen to the Christians who have died *so you will not be full of sorrow like people who have no hope.* For since we believe that Jesus died and was raised to life again, we also believe that when Jesus comes, God will bring back with Jesus all the Christians who have died. I can tell you this directly from the Lord. We who are still living when the Lord returns will not rise to meet him ahead of those who are in their graves. For the Lord Himself will come down from heaven with a commanding shout, with the call of the archangel, and with the trumpet call of God. First, all of the Christians who have died will rise from their graves. Then, together with them, we who are still alive and remain on the earth will be caught up in the clouds to meet the Lord in the air and remain with Him forever. *So comfort and encourage each other with these words* (NLT, emphasis added).

I emphasized the two lines from this passage that stand out to me. What words can I say to comfort and encourage the Hoppels? I can scarcely think clearly.

Paul does not say, "Don't grieve," but rather says, "Don't grieve as others do who have no hope." Of course you are grieving – death is ugly, and your loss is real. But the difference for you is the *hope*.

I will always remember Robert's

allegiance to Christ. He was a child of God. He could not cope with life, and in despair threw himself on the mercy of Christ. The truth of the gospel is forgiveness freely offered through Christ. Christ's sacrifice was sufficient to cover all transgressions.

To my knowledge, there are few cases of suicide recorded in the Bible (Judges 9 – Abimelech; Judges 16 – Samson; 2 Samuel 17 – Ahithophel; 1 Kings 16 – Zimri; 1 Samuel 31 – Saul and his armor-bearer; and Matthew 27 – Judas Iscariot), and in none of these instances is there a single word of condemnation of these men for the way they died.

Whether they were afflicted with delusions of grandeur and power like Zimri and Abimelech, or were remorseful traitors like Judas and Ahithophel, or divinely-appointed leaders like Samson and Saul and his faithful armor-bearer, the biblical account records no negative judgment on them in describing their acts of suicide. Instead, in every case, the deaths are treated simply as any other death would be. Death may come in many different ways; all deaths bring sorrow and despair.

Jesus said, "My sheep recognize my

voice; I know them, and they follow Me. I give them eternal life and they will never perish. No one will snatch them away from Me" (John 10:27-28). This is our sustaining hope and strength. The Gospel is the Good News that proclaims mercy and grace. The Christ of the Gospel is a Christ who knows and understands. May you be comforted and encouraged with these words.

You may be too numb to think about the future, so "hold on to" Isaiah 41:10 in the days ahead. We promise you, it is true and time-tested: "Don't be afraid, for I am with you. Do not be dismayed, for I am your God. I will strengthen you. I will help you. I will uphold you with my victorious right hand."

Don't be reticent to talk about suicide and to admit to yourselves and others that this event has been a part of your lives. Don't let any shame, anger, or guilt that could flood in upon you drive you away from the help you may need.

The deep pain you are feeling is as if your whole life is torn in shreds. Nothing but your own loss is of any importance to you right now. So don't fight it. Your friends and family will understand. You are never alone – God is as close as your own tears.

Your friends and family are with you, too. In the midst of our own routines, we will be praying for you, and you will receive help.

There is no shortcut to grief, but be assured, we are thinking of you with loving and suffering hearts.

>Dick and Ardie Nielsen
>Pastor and family friends

★★★★★

Here I Am
Written by Rob Hoppel

Here I am, oh God, Your son.
I hear Your call and I am one,
With Your Spirit I will go;
So speak to me.

I call upon You on my knees.
You pick me up and deliver me.
I will glorify Your Name;
So speak to me.

You give me destiny in youth.
You give me hope, I find in You.
With Your motive I see truth;
So speak to me.

Chorus
Oh Lord, my God.
On holy ground I kneel before the cross.
Oh Lord, my God.
Peaceful, cleansing spirits overwhelm me.

★★★★★

As I Am
Written by Rob H.

Verse

Will you restore evermore my life, my life?
Can I enjoy furthermore by light, by light?
I want to live my life by You, by You.
I want You by my side, it's true, it's true.

Chorus
I'm just another broken spirit.
I'm on my knees. Please break me.
Then pick me up and hold me in Your arms.
Thank you for loving me. As I am.

Verse

It makes me sad to hear the lies, the lies.
I wish I could understand. I try, I try.

Then you came bounding to me with love, with love.
A thing that I never knew, I trust, I trust.

★★★★★

August 4, 1985

I will never forget the day and hour. I had been in labor for three days and the midwives told me that it was finally time to get serious. This child was not going to come without my concentrated effort on labor and delivery and nothing else. I had tried to speed things along with a few walks around the blocks. When I finally checked into the Bethesda Maternity Center thinking that the real thing was close at hand, the midwives gave me a stern lecture about socializing with my friends and family that had come to participate in the birth of my second child.

When the admonition was over, they whisked me out the door to the track of Walter Johnson High School next door for some power walking to get those contractions going. Steve, my husband, and I walked and walked and walked. Finally, the pains were long enough and hard enough to go back inside and bunker down for the real thing. At 10:05 p.m., the real thing came. Robert James Alexander Hoppel made his appearance into the world for all to adore!

We chose a birth center over a hospital because we wanted Robert's birth to be special. We had known friends from California who had delivered their babies at home and the stories we had heard of the comfort of being at home as opposed to a more sterile environment of a hospital appealed to us. Robert's sister, Rebekah, was born in a hospital in California three years earlier and it was a wonderful experience. But we wanted this second birth to be different, so when we heard of the birth center with all the comforts of home as well as the availability of medical treatment if needed, we decided to go with it. And we were glad we did. It was a delight to have so many friends and family close at hand to witness the birth of our second child and first son, Robert. He came into the world with blond hair, blue eyes, and he was healthy, happy and raring to go!

Two years later, our holiday letter to friends and family had this to say about the bundle of energy we had graciously been given by God to raise:

Robert and Rebekah are doing just fine. Robert just turned two and is a typical two-year-old lad. A sustaining word for me from the Lord has been that Robert is my "diamond," a "diamond in the rough" giving me hope for the future and encouragement for the present. He's very active!

For three years after Robert was born, our life was a happy one. Steve was a self-employed painting contractor doing well in business and I was preparing to home school my then three-year-old daughter, Rebekah. Life was fun. We lived in a small but cozy house in Cabin John, Maryland, and I was also starting to build a typing business, determined to be the stay-at-home mom my heart had always been set on being.

In July of 1988, a car accident caused by an elderly woman running a red light brought major complications to the pregnancy of our third-born child, complications that ultimately changed the world of each member of our young and growing family of four. Our son, David, was born two weeks premature and was acutely ill. The doctors did not know if he would live.

We had to surrender this fragile life to God, knowing that David belonged to Him and that He could do with Him as He pleased. When David was two days old, our pastor at the time visited his hospital bed, anointed him with oil, and prayed for his recovery. Three weeks later David was well enough to be discharged from the hospital, but the neonatologists warned us that he faced an uncertain future. They could give us no guarantees that David would ever walk or talk.

Our lives for the next five years proved to be a roller coaster of a ride, discovering at 18 months of age that David, while battling life-threatening pneumonias and other upper respiratory infections, had a brain injury causing ongoing seizures and slow development. Special schools, therapy, and intense emergency medical treatment consumed our time, energy, and emotions for several years. Though the Lord most certainly sustained us through those uncertain times, the stress of years of crisis management took its toll. Depression set in that I was too weary to overcome in my natural strength. I sought medical treatment and began a course of anti-depressant therapy that helped to relieve my pain for nearly eighteen months.

In 1994, I was pregnant with our fourth child and felt an urgency to discontinue all medication I was on for depression. The Lord spoke to me one evening as I was lying on the couch in our living room, crying out to Him for relief from the deep, dark feelings of hopelessness and despair. I remembered a Scripture that spoke of "a garment of praise for a spirit of heaviness" (Isaiah 61:3) and I started to praise and worship the Lord in a way I had never praised and worshiped before. The spirit of heaviness lifted and I was able to get through the remainder of my pregnancy with Joshua medication-free. It wasn't easy, but it was possible. God's Word proved true to me at a time of desperate need.

The battle we fought on behalf of David subsided and came to a peaceful calm in 1995 when he was finally well enough to enter regular school. It was the same year that Robert started to do poorly in school and we had to figure out how we could help him get back on the road to academic success. We decided to withdraw him from the small private school he had been attending and homeschool him as we had successfully done with his sister a few years prior. Robert did not adjust as well to homeschooling as we had hoped and after eighteen months, we enrolled him in the local public school in the hope he could utilize his growing musical talents that were a source of strength and delight to him and all who knew him well. Robert had hope for his future as he documented in an English Essay he wrote for school:

> I, Robert J. Hoppel, am an 8th grade student at T.W. Pyle Middle School in Bethesda, MD. There are many goals I hope to achieve in life. I have a lot of strengths and weaknesses that affect my goals in life. I have played violin and drums since I was five. I am organized most of the time and I am all around hyper and active at times. I also have some fatal weaknesses: My left hand is weak, I am at times moody. I get disorganized fast. I am fearful of things I have not done and I am cowardly about some things. The strengths will more than likely help me with my later on goals. And I hope I can overcome my weaknesses.

Unfortunately, Robert had a difficult time adjusting to public school. He kept a journal documenting his struggles and conversations he would have with the Lord. He didn't feel as if he fit in and he often cried out to the Lord for answers to the many struggles he would have as evidenced by the following entry in his journal:

My Child, I am with you.

The unjust blood cries to Me on these grounds and I will not forsake them.

Pray for the souls of these lost people. Pray they turn from their wicked ways and claim my truth.

Do not be lonely. I am here with you, son.

Do not hear when you are called crazy because of Me. For when the tables of time turn, all will profess My truth.

Love and honor your teachers even though they teach against My ways. Pity them that they know not the freedom they could have in Me.

Do not strive to be popular among these people. This will only make you forget My ways.

Let all see My love through your life. Love is patient, kind, short to anger ... show all these things to everyone, even those who look at you in disgust.

Do not be angry with things that happen to you here. Do you not think these things I control? Are you angry with what I do with your life? Likewise, rejoice when evil is done to you and you do not take revenge.

Temptation will always come but it is a simple choice you need to make. To live for Me or to live for the desires of your own heart.

Pray in the Spirit through these halls that I might soak this property with My Presence.

His freshman year of high school was especially difficult. At age 13, he was angry. He wasn't doing well in school and the consequences of him acting out were severe. In January, we took him to the hospital to see if there was any physiological explanation for his increasingly aggressive change in behavior.

Robert's anger became worse and he started trying to solve his conflicts with irrational and impulsive acts – swallowing a bottle of pills in April and slitting his wrists in June – a day before his sister's graduation from high school. Three days later, he drank a bottle of champagne, mixing alcohol with medication he had been on for ADHD – an act of irrational impulsivity that nearly claimed his life.

Robert remained in the hospital for five days where he was watched and diagnosed as manically depressed. He was released on the condition that he would receive weekly counseling and continue his medication that now included a major anti-depressant. Here are a few more journal entries:

> *I don't think I'm getting it. Something is not right ... I want so much to be able to have You and Your ways on my mind constantly, but I can't. Please help me ... talk to me, Lord ... please talk to me.*

"Do not be deceived by the lies that have been presented to you ... Why do you search for ways to be different? If anything, be different because of what I am doing through you … do not do things to give people the impression you are "bad" or have some deep dark secret that haunts your mind and soul. But act like yourself. Nothing more, nothing less … do not care what other people think of you. Care what I think of you. Keep Me in mind at all times and remember the paradise I have in store for those who claim Me.

At age 14, Robert in desperation of heart, soul, and mind, cried out to God. Robert was sorry for what he had done and he began to surrender his life, once again, to God. He began reading his Bible daily, understanding the importance of filling his mind with God's thoughts and ways, and casting away the thoughts and ways of the world that had been infiltrating his heart and mind with devastating consequences. He threw away the CDs and lyrics of the music of evil-driven "artists" who were poisoning his mind with unmerciful suggestions of rage, murder, and suicide.

He willingly gave himself to the counseling process, mandated by the hospital he was released from, and what we witnessed over the course of the next year, with a few minor setbacks in between, was "a transformation" in his counselor's own words. Here is an entry of a dialogue he had with the Lord.

Lord, I don't know what's wrong. Why can't I write songs? What do You have for me? Please start to show me Your will for my life. Thank You for helping me with my grades. Please don't let my mind try to fulfill a desire with other things besides You. Please let me feel happy with what I am doing and strive to do what's right. I love you, Lord. Thank You for helping me. Please speak to me about these things.

Things come in time. Do not strive to accomplish in one day what I will bring out in your lifetime. Be at peace. When the time is right, I will give these things to you. You cannot take them now as your own.

Thank You, Lord, I understand. Thank You!

Lord, I want to know You more. Lord, speak to me through Your Word, and let me be at peace. Let me be humble. And give me the faith and boldness to be a light to others. Lord, please make me into the person that my future spouse needs. Please let me live by Your Will and not mine. I lay my life at Your feet, and I pray You do what You may with it. Please start revealing what You would like me to do as a career. Lord, I want to play music. I really do. Please start to show me today what You want with my life. I love You and I praise You.

Lord, take my sins, I'm sorry, please forgive me. Let Your Spirit come down on me.

God, I know You are real. Show me that You're real. Nothing about You is false. Satan is trying to lie to me. Please! Tell him to leave me. Don't let the blanket of doubt come over the peace I've found in You. Please ... "

CHAPTER 2
SMILE IN THE RAIN

Family Friend
June 20, 2001

Oh, Jenny, this is unreal. I will be praying, especially that the enemy not divide you and Steve right now. You need each other more than ever.

Jenny, I am going to just share my heart. If anything I say offends you, please forgive me, but I would like to share some things with you … they are things I would say if I were there personally and we could sit together and talk about this.

Ultimately, I think suicide is a spirit, and in Robert's case, I think that spirit just absolutely overwhelmed him. Yes, I completely agree with you that the Lord just lifted Robert up to Himself. Robert must have been struggling so hard to keep that spirit/spirits from invading his thoughts, etc. Sure, it was probably made worse by the lack of medication, conversations that upset him, etc., but ultimately, it was the enemy.

But I also believe Psalm 139 is true – that "our days are ordained for us" – and for whatever reasons, the Lord allowed this in Robert's life. But at the same time, an understanding of spiritual warfare is needed now. Think about the man in the Bible who was tormented by the group of spirits who identified themselves as Legion. Those spirits had to go somewhere, so they went into the swine. But look at the force with which they entered the swine. They overpowered the swine so much that they were hurled headlong over the cliff. Doesn't that say something about the powerful nature of these spirits? I think it does. Robert's struggle must have been similarly unimaginable.

Jenny, if I were there, I would band the parents together, and begin some very earnest prayer and fasting on behalf of the children. I would also suggest some major repenting for the decision of Roe v. Wade because the Lord spoke to me that it is directly linked to the reason why young people are committing suicide. Remember that word I shared with you? I will send you another copy, but I want to finish my remarks, for whatever they may be worth.

Here is the word, Jenny, that I submitted to The Call DC which you heard them use during the repentance phase of that day. Since Robert's death, I have sensed from the Lord, to keep on repenting for this until this is no longer the law of the land.

This is the perspective and prayer that the Lord gave me in the fall of 1997, just a few short months before the 25th anniversary of the passing of Roe v. Wade. I never knew why I kept focusing on 25 and under, but when the Lord spoke to me, I completely understood the link to a decision that was 25 years old.

For several years, I began asking the Lord again and again why so many young people, especially those 25 years and younger, were choosing to commit suicide. *Why, Lord, why?* One day, in the fall of 1997, He answered me.

> You (your generation of Baby Boomers) opened the door with Roe v. Wade. With that decision, you told this generation (25 and under/now 28 and under) that they were not wanted, disposable,

inconvenient, not viable, and if that wasn't enough, you went one step further and you labeled this generation … Generation X … and told them that they were nothing, and there was nothing left for them. And my son added, "And they became a fatherless generation because it is called 'a woman's right to choose.'"

As a result, the Lord continued to say,

"This Supreme Court decision of Roe v. Wade has become a door of access that was opened to the enemy to begin to wipe out this generation. This decision has become something like a sentence of death that is now hanging over them as a generation. If the enemy cannot get this generation at conception, through abortion, then, just as they are beginning their life as a young person, and beginning to step into the destiny and purpose that I had for them since the beginning of time, the enemy, who is the father of all lies, will speak to them and tell them that their life was not worth living and many believe that lie and commit suicide. And now, they are even beginning to take the lives of their own generation through massacres like Columbine."

This is what the Lord then led me to pray over our sons and daughters.

To our precious sons and daughters,

Please forgive my generation of Baby Boomers for allowing the decision of Roe v. Wade to be passed by the Supreme Court and become the law of the land. Please forgive us for our silence on your behalf and for not realizing the devastating effect and long-term consequences that this decision would have on you as a generation.

We ask You, Heavenly Father, come now, and cover our sin with the blood of Jesus. We ask you, Father, to lay the ax to the root of the door of access that this decision gave the enemy to think that somehow he now had the right to wipe you out as a generation. We ask you, Father, to cancel this sentence of death that has been illegally hanging over you as a generation, because of this decision. Father, please come now, and with Your strong right arm of deliverance, sever **any** and **all** effects of Roe v. Wade on our sons and daughters, in the name of Jesus.

We also ask you, our sons and daughters, to forgive us for allowing partial birth abortions to also be the law of the land. We say no to the effect of that decision on you as a generation, and we ask You, Father, to sever all effects of that decision, in the name of Jesus.

And please forgive us for labeling you Generation X for that is not who you are. You are prophetically called the Generation of the Righteous. You are not Generation Y either, but you are called to be a generation of worshipers who will worship the living God in Spirit and in truth.

We speak life over you now as a generation, in the name of Jesus. As a generation, you will not experience only a partial birth of God's purpose in your lives, but we call you forth as a generation to come full term into the destiny and purpose that the Father has had for you since the beginning of time. Father, we ask you now, in the name of Jesus, to restore this generation to their rightful place in history.

We bless you, as a generation, with the promises found in Jeremiah 29:11-14:

> 'For I know the plans that I have for you, declares the Lord, plans for welfare and not for calamity to give you a future and a hope. Then you will call upon Me and come and pray to Me and I will listen to you. And you will seek Me and find Me, when you search for Me with all your heart. And I will be found by you, declares the Lord and I will restore your fortunes and will gather you from all the nations and from the places where I have driven you, declares the

> Lord and I will bring you back to the place from where I sent you into exile."

Jenny, when I was there for Robert's service, I asked the Lord to give me some divine appointments. Robert's friend sat next to me on Friday night, and I was able to say some comforting things to him. Then I met another friend of Robert's and blessed her with Jeremiah 29. I just felt compelled in my spirit to speak life over these kids who are so shaken by what has happened.

Ultimately, the enemy wants to wipe them out, but he is going to have to get past those of us who will stand in the gap and say no, that this generation does not belong to him. The battle is real, that is what Robert's death has shown me, and we better take it seriously. The enemy means business, and he is after their very lives. If Robert's death is used by God to wake up a sleeping generation (ours), then he will not have died in vain.

★★★★★

This picture of Rob on the following page was taken at the Call D.C., Saturday, September 2, 2000 on the grounds of the Capitol Mall in Washington, D.C. Thousands of parents and teens gathered on these historic grounds for the purpose of repentance, reconciliation, and prayer.

Robert's attendance at this historic event was a miracle. The year 2000 had been very tough for our family. He had truly come to offer up prayers of repentance alongside his dad who attended the youth rally with him. At the time the picture was taken, it was raining. Towards the end of the day, the heavens opened up and it started to pour. People were scrambling for their umbrellas or running for cover. One man in our group had the brilliant idea of lifting the blue tarp the kids had brought for ground cover up in the air and positioned the teens at each corner to make a circus tent-type cover that would keep everyone dry.

Robert got a big kick out of this. He really enjoyed the concept of doing something unique and daring for the sake of the whole. Some kids could have kept dry using

the few umbrellas that were brought to the event, but everyone was able to keep dry with a few resources and a lot of ingenuity. The kids moved through the Mall to the Metro station in one unified group, singing and laughing the whole way. We had friends attending the conference from California and though the sheer number of people at one place at one time made personal connection impossible, I asked later on the phone if they had seen the kids under the big blue tarp moving through the crowd. She said that she had, and I excitedly claimed, "That was Robert! That was our youth group!" I even think they got TV coverage. We had all learned to smile … even in the rain.

★★★★★

Smile in the Rain
Written by Rob. H

Verse

*You looked out the back window and stared at me
I was tired and cold but you did not care
I just wish you could love me like I do you
There is so much you cannot do*

Chorus

*Why don't you turn to me? Why don't you look at me?
Standing in the rain
Why don't you turn around? Why don't you smile at me?
A smile in the rain*

Verse

I look out and I see the moon
Stars so bright, doom is near
The rain will come through here, though I fear
But I will [I will] stay here

Jennifer Hoppel

Illustration designed for Memorial Service Brochure
by friend and fellow worship team member, Karin Slawinski

CHAPTER 3
The Homegoing Service

Dr. L. Daniel Wolfe, Pastor
June 3, 2001

You know last night was a very important meeting for us when we met with all the youth and the parents here in the auditorium. And it was a powerful time of expressing our feelings. And this helped us with being able to honestly release our feelings of grief and sadness and sorrow and mourning over this death.

But there is one focus that I would like to express that we should all have, today and in the coming days. It's something that our *minds* will focus on, even though our emotions can be tangled and can be up and down through these coming days and weeks and months. I want to encourage us to keep our *minds* focused, as the Scriptures say in a certain way. And so I have this passage from Isaiah 26 where the Word of the Lord is this:

> "You will keep in perfect peace, him or her whose mind is steadfast because they trust in You. Trust in the Lord forever, for the Lord, the Lord is the Rock eternal."

This is the Word I believe that God has for the family and all the friends who are here with us today. Because God is bigger than any of this. And our minds need to be very focused. And [we need to] trust in God. There is a great mystery in many ways about this death. And we've all asked, 'What if, what if, what if?' And when I got the call on my cell phone, I shouted, 'Oh, no. This is something we never wanted to see.'

But God is bigger. And even though there are mysteries that surround this death, there is a Rock that's eternal and, if our minds would be steadfastly trusting in God, God said that peace will come.

As I was driving up to Greenbrier with Janice to be with the family and the friends at the campground, I had an unusual experience with God. God began to speak peace into my heart. I thought, *I'm going to be real agitated on this trip.* This is one of the most unusual words I've ever received in my life and I'm on my way up with Janice when God surrounded me with peace. As I sat in my car, I said to Janice, "I feel like God is telling me that He's bigger than this and He's going to grant peace to everybody. And that it's going to come from Him if we trust Him with all of our hearts."

You know, peace is not the absence of conflict or the absence of any storm. Peace is that rest and confidence in God right in the midst of it. When everything is taking place. And when the emotions are really tangled up. And when the thoughts come. Peace comes from trusting God who's bigger than anything that we can ever experience here in this life. It says in Philippians and this is another Word from God:

> Don't be anxious about everything, but in every way, by prayers and petitions and supplications, let your requests be made known to God. And the peace of God which passes all understanding, will guard your hearts and minds through Christ Jesus (Philippians 4:6-7).

You know we are trying to figure everything out. We'll never figure this all out, will we? But God says that if we would let our hearts go to Him that He would come back on us with peace. It would bypass our minds because our minds would not be able to figure this all out. This is a great word from God, that peace would be the result as we trust in the Lord with all of our hearts.

And the Lord said a second thing to me on the way up to Greenbrier. He said, "Make sure that this is a life-changing experience for everybody." Because we're the ones that are here. And we're the ones who still have life to live. And the Lord said, "Make sure that it's life-changing." It can't be like a week or two, or a month in which our emotions are touched by God when we face the ultimate reality of life and death. But let it be something that will change us the rest of our lives, so we will never be quite as casual again with God and with His Word and with the things He wants to say to us.

Also, that we would never be casual with our parents. That we would have hearts that are tender, submitted to those who love us and care about us. That we would never be casual with our friends who try to tell us the best way to go. And that we would never be casual with the world system and the culture of this day that would like to squeeze us right into its mold. That somehow we, as believers, would say, "God, help us to live in such a way that we will be saved from anything like this that could ever come upon us again."

Peace in the midst of it all is from God if we trust in Him who is bigger than it all. May God bless you all. Thank you for coming. Amen.

★★★★★

To Worship Our God
Written by Rob H.

Verse

I lift my voice to my Lord who loves me more than I can say
So what is it that makes me sing? That pushes me to say

Chorus

Lift your voice to the Lord. Let creation sing
In unison, with one voice to worship

To worship our God

Verse

I'm needy Lord, I need Your voice to guide me on my way
Your steadfast will for my life. Please mold it into mine.

★★★★★

On January 28, 2003, I was crossing the historic Union Arch Bridge in our neighborhood to pick up a friend of our youngest son for a play date. I noticed that yellow police tape had blocked the footpath portion of this narrow, one-lane bridge. As I crossed in my car to the other side, I noticed two police cars and what looked to be a homicide detective hanging together, obviously discussing something serious. I noticed a third man peering through a chain link fence over the Clara Barton Highway below. He just kept peering, and I wondered and prayed.

On the way back to our house, I pulled over to talk to a man parked on the other side. I could see the police had closed down the highway below and wanted to know the reason why. The man told me that they had found a body and that the police were conducting an investigation. My body felt numb as I asked him if it was a suicide. The man looked at me and said that it was too early to tell but that they suspected that it was. I raced home to call the local fire department to see if they could tell me more. Something in me had to know.

The officer on the phone said that he could not divulge any details concerning the closure of the bridge and the highway below it. I asked him point blank, "Officer, can you tell me this? Was it a suicide?" And the officer softly replied that they were investigating a possible suicide jump off the one-lane bridge less than three minutes from our home.

My kind neighbor who had lived next door for fifty years was able to tell me more. His brother had gone down to see the body. He reported an "older man" had jumped to his death just hours before, though his identity had not been released. And I knew that it wouldn't be released. I had asked Ranger Boback a year or so after Robert's death if there had been anything in the paper on the incident involving our church's camping trip and Robert's suicide. He told me that the press usually doesn't report suicides for obvious reasons. The press didn't report this suicide either even though the investigation blocked a major artery to the nation's capital during rush hour for several hours. I wanted to know who died and I desperately wanted to know why.

I found myself, as Pastor Dan had said at Robert's memorial service, trying to figure it out. Why did this man, whose identity I didn't even know, end his life this way? Is there anything I could have done to help him come to a different conclusion in life? What goes on in the heart and mind of a person contemplating ending their life?

Robert's memorial service was beautiful. The church was overflowing with family and friends. The pastors had anticipated this and asked to hold the service over to the following Saturday so that all who wanted to attend would be free to do so. The week prior remains a blur to my memory – in fact the entire ordeal remains a blur. Food and flowers and friends arrived to our door before we even returned home from the campgrounds. The smallest of details were worked out by friends and staff of the church we attended. So many decisions to make in so short a time.

A suicide death doesn't give much time to prepare so the responses that came to help us along were heartfelt and genuine. This so helped ease the pain. All I remember is abundance – of food, of flowers, of cards, of love and concern showered down on our family. Our God is an abundant God and He showered His blessings down on us like rain.

The people who spoke at the service were close to us and their words were meaningful. These people knew Robert and they knew his pain. And now they were in pain themselves and they did their best in the midst of their pain to honor our son. For this we will be forever grateful. We know that love given from a heart filled with pain is the purest of love and we appreciated their sacrifice. Our son was honored and remembered in spite of all the pain he had caused. Here is another one of the entries in his journal:

> *Lord, I love You. I long for more of You. I want my life to resemble the great work You do in me.*

Lord, let me love as You love me.

Let me serve, as You serve me.

Forgive me of my sins, and help me to forgive.

Let me be patient with others, as You are patient with me.

Let me not go through one minute without loving and thinking and praising You.

Lord, please forgive me for these past days. I was angry, Lord, I felt I needed something that You did not want to give me. I wanted people to accept me. I wanted to accept myself. I wanted to be happy. I wanted to be successful.

Lord, all of these things I know You have in store for my life, please help me to live Your will for my life. Please begin to show me what that will is.

From Angels' Holy Hands

Sketch by John Kumnick

CHAPTER 4
Ranger Boback

Comments by Rebekah Hoppel, Robert's Sister

"Excerpts from My Prayer Journal: January 3, 2000"

As I've been praying for Robert, pouring out my heart to God to touch his life during this time of trial, the Holy Spirit came upon me and gave me a complete peace. Robert is my inheritance. His soul is my inheritance. I never really saw the value in gold or precious stones that everyone seems to value, but my reward isn't really gold or silver. It's people. Their souls. Their eternal bliss. Eternal communion with God if they surrender their hearts and lives to Jesus Christ.

We have a Creator who values so highly the eternally important stuff: Robert, the Nepali people, Juan, the countless children who die on the streets each day. They are my treasure. One pair of eyes is worth more than a castle full of diamonds. Wow, Father, thank You so much. Help me that on that judgment day, I can give all my inheritance, including Robert, back to You.

One of the things I most looked forward to for the future was Robert's rehearsal dinner for his wedding. Being the big sister, I just couldn't wait to make that perfectly humiliating speech in front of all the new in-laws. I even had a picture that he hated of course, of him wearing white spandex pants that I was going to blow up to life-sized proportions. I was going to say how Robert meant so much to me. How difficult it was going to be to give him into the arms of someone else.

Robert's birth is my first memory. I remember being at home, begging my grandparents to take me to go see him right away. But they said we had to wait.

I remember all of our Suzuki violin rehearsals together, listening and playing, and listening and listening again, until we felt all those 'Mississippi Hot Dogs' were going to come out of our noses. I remember all the times he let me dress him up as a girl to play house. But then, instead of acting properly during tea time, he pretended to be a rat and chased me around the dining room table.

I remember swimming in the freezing ocean, only to go roll around in the hot sand. I remember him sneaking up behind me to squeeze my stomach and make me squeal. I remember how when he went to Austria, he had run out of money, but instead of saving his last few dollars to buy lunch, he bought me a pencil with a crystal on the end.

I remember when we went rock climbing together and he was so brave when he fell. He made jokes the entire time the doctor was stitching him up.

I remember him singing me that song he wrote for me for my graduation. How he could capture in song exactly how he felt.

I remember him coming to Marymount and showing off to every college girl in sight.

I remember sitting and just listening to him worship. Sometimes we sang together, just praising God. I remember all our talks. How so many times he told me to be honest and sincere about everything all the time. And I remember that day, Sunday, May 27, 2001, when he looked up at me as he was worshiping at the church service. How our eyes met and we connected. How perfect that moment was.

But I don't know what else I would have gotten to say. Because that was my last memory.

Not only do I have to go on making memories without him, but now I must wait to see him once again.

Well, you know, even though I'll never get to make that speech, right now, as a Christian, Robert is the bride of Christ. He is waiting for the rest of us to join him at the Marriage Supper of the Lamb. So now, Robert, as you're sitting at that Banquet Table, for your wedding present, I pray that all these people here, in this room, and then all the people in Romania, who commit their lives to Jesus Christ, will become your inheritance. I pray that on that last day, you will look around and see us as your treasure. Not gold or jewels, but precious, precious people.

I love you, Robert. And through all this pain of having to wait once again, I thank God for you, my inheritance.

Ranger Boback called six months after Robert's death and asked if we wanted to see the site where our son took his life. At first the thought repulsed me and was similar to how I felt when we were asked if we wanted to view the body. I didn't want to see the body and I didn't want to see the tree. But Ranger Boback was ready when we were and one day, nearly eighteen months later, I called him on his cell phone and told him I was ready. I wanted to see the tree.

My husband, Steve, and second son, David, were already camping at the park. They hadn't been back to Greenbrier since Memorial Day weekend one year ago. David was anxious to return, as was his dad. I wasn't so eager and stayed home to clean house and watch Joshua play with his friends.

Steve called 10:00 Saturday morning and asked me if I would be willing to bring out some things they had forgotten. Greenbrier State Park is only 45 minutes away and I was able to break away from housework and deliver some amenities that would make their stay there more comfortable. Besides, Joshua had regretted his decision not to go with them and asked if he could spend the second night at the park.

When I got off the phone with Steve, a thought popped into my mind: "What would you think about visiting the tree today?" It hadn't crossed my mind since Ranger Boback called six months ago. With the thought came an awareness that I was ready. It was part of the closure process that Steve wanted to make when I was ready. I realized it had to be done.

Arriving at the campsite, I told Steve that I had called Ranger Boback who happened to be on duty that weekend and was making preparations to help us find the tree where Robert took his life. Ranger Boback needed to gather some supplies but said that if we went down to the Visitors Center when we were ready, he would meet us there and escort us through the woods to the site.

Ranger Boback had gone to great trouble to mark the site for us. He needed a map, compass, and metal detector since the tree was deep inside the woods, off the beaten path of trails. Ranger Boback knew one year ago that we would never find the tree again if he didn't mark it off and draw a map to help him find it again – just in case we ever asked.

We started retracing the steps we guessed our son had taken that fateful night one year prior. My husband had taken off running trying to catch him as he ran off our campsite and down the road, leaping over the guardrail and into the woods. He lost sight of him quickly and wasn't sure which direction he had taken. Steve came back to the campsite convinced that Robert just needed to "blow off some steam" and that he would return later that evening after having some time to cool off. The last words we heard him say were, "I'm tired, I'm wet, and I haven't taken my medicine in five days!"

Ranger Boback explained to us that there would have been no way we could have known which direction he would have taken. And he didn't blame us for waiting until morning to contact the authorities to help. He said that kids run off all the time and that even if we had called the night before, they wouldn't have been able to start a thorough search party until daybreak anyway. As he followed his map and confirmed the direction we were taking by the detection of the metal pegs he had so thoughtfully driven into the ground one year ago, the Ranger solemnly took us deep into the woods and up a steep hill to the tree our son climbed to end his life.

The tree wasn't anything that I expected it to be. In fact, it didn't seem to be a tree at all. It was like a thick limb, sprouting from the ground at a 45-degree angle, an easy climb – and not very tall. In fact, Ranger Boback told us that had Robert placed the belt that he looped around the tree just two inches in either direction, his life would have been spared. Two inches up, he explained, the tree limb was totally rotten and the weight of his body would have snapped the limb in two. Two inches down, Robert's feet would have touched the ground and his attempt to take his life would have been thwarted.

My daughter's immediate questions when she heard the devastating news was "Why? Why did God allow this to happen? Why didn't God stop him?" Seeing the tree brought remarkable closure to this question for us. God could have easily interrupted this plan, for this was a preventable accident. The fact is that God didn't prevent, but rather He allowed Robert to position himself, at night, in the dark, in a frenzied state of mind, at precisely the right location.

I don't think Robert could have planned this – he was too tired, too cold, too upset to truly think this through. Though we do not understand why, we know beyond a shadow of a doubt that God allowed this tragedy to happen. And we are at peace with this. We do not know why but we know that God loved Robert very, very much and He allowed him to die. He allowed him to enter a rest, a peace that passes understanding, not here with us, but with Him, in heaven. Robert's heart longed for this. He wanted to be with God.

★★★★★

Journal Entry, Robert Hoppel

Talk to me, Lord, please talk to me. Show me what You want. Build my faith in You and let me be passionate for You.

Matthew 3:17, 'This is my Son, whom I love; with him I am well pleased.'

Lord, let me please You. Let my actions, my life be pleasing to You.

Matthew 5:4, 'Blessed are those who mourn, for they will be comforted.'

Matthew 5:6, 'Blessed are those who hunger and thirst for righteousness, for they will be filled.'

Matthew 5:11, "Blessed are You when people insult you, persecute you and falsely say all kinds of evil against you because of Me. Rejoice and be glad, because great is your reward in heaven…"

Lord, thank You for showing me these things. Please let them stay on my mind.

CHAPTER 5
MARS

Carry my burden when I can't walk myself. The road is too long and I'm not that strong. And right now I need your help. The dust is hot. It's blinding me. This road is rough. Please carry my burden. It will be enough to carry me. To carry me home. Sometimes I can't find my feet and there are stones in the road. They seem intent on tripping me. Carry me. And carry my burden, too. There are too many miles to count. And this journey seems like a lifetime. And the joy is often mingled with sadness. But then joy again and joy in the morning.

Family Friend
June 3, 2021

★★★★★

Take Me Away (unfinished)
Written by Rob H.

Take me away, I want to leave
Sweep me off my feet and take me far away
I'm begging you now, I don't want to stay
Here with all this sorrow and pain
So give me wings, that I may fly away
Away from myself … away from my mind
Or make them like You, honest and true
So I don't want to fly away from here

Look Back in Time
Written by Robert H.

I'm trying to stay alive
Please make my mind revived
I'm trying to see what You see
I'm just trying to see what You see
I'm just trying to survive

So take my thoughts aside
And put them in beside
The Truth and Peace of Your Mind
And then I'll be alive

I never knew his real name. I just knew what Robert called him and how he laughed when he remembered how Mars tried to escape in his wheelchair every time the nurses buzzed someone into the psychiatric ward on the seventh floor of Suburban Hospital in Bethesda, Maryland. I knew Suburban Hospital well. My father had died of lung cancer there in 1991 and to help myself through the grieving process of losing a parent I dearly loved, I went to work there as a switchboard operator and then a security guard. I enjoyed being a security guard. I got to walk the halls of every floor in the hospital, including the psychiatric ward, making my rounds, and praying for the patients as I passed their rooms and tried to feel their pain.

There was nothing funny about being on Floor 7, but I was blessed that my son found something to smile about in the midst of this terrible situation. I will never forget the day we first took him to Suburban Hospital. My heart was trembling. These were unchartered waters for us but we didn't know what else to do. Our son was uncontrollably angry. The police and local teen crisis center had advised us to take him to the hospital for evaluation.

All we told him when we checked in at the emergency room was that he was angry. They sent him right to Floor 7 – the Psych Ward as we used to call it in my security guard days. When Robert was admitted, it had a more sophisticated name – "Center for Emotional and Psychological Development" – but to us, it was Floor 7 – where the psychos lived and my son had just been admitted for medical issues involving bouts of uncontrollable anger.

I remember seeing him lying on his bed. He was afraid. He didn't want to stay there. He begged us to take him home but we told him that he was just there for testing, which was true. We wanted to see if he had a brain tumor or get any insight that might help explain the behavior he had been exhibiting the previous three months. We needed some help – and we needed it quickly.

Three days later, Robert was discharged with the diagnosis of Severe Untreated Attention Deficit Disorder. This was not a surprise to us. Robert had been diagnosed with Attention Deficit Disorder when he was five years old. The psychiatrist at the time was not totally sure of his diagnosis but said we could try ritalyn if we wanted to see if it would help Robert pay closer attention at school. Robert didn't like the idea of being on medication – not even at age five – but we tried it to see if it would help. Not noticing a significant difference in his behavior, we discontinued it when Robert entered the second grade.

At age seven, we tried something new to try to help Robert stay focused. One day, Robert asked if he could study drums and we thought it might be a good activity to help him focus his energies. Robert was already a fine musician. He had been studying violin since he was three and a half, and was doing well for his age at both violin and piano. The thought of adding a third instrument was a bit overwhelming, but he was very passionate and adamant about it. I remember the day I questioned him to make sure that it wasn't going to be just a passing interest. He burst into tears and said as best he could articulate it, "I don't know, Mom. I can't explain it. It's just in my heart to do it."

At age nine, Robert started playing drums for our church's worship team. At 13 he was traveling with the District of Columbia Youth Orchestra on a ten-day tour of Vienna, Austria to celebrate a centennial. It was a big event and an honor for him to have been chosen to go at such a young age.

Robert loved his drums, which he played with passion. As I saw him lying on the bed of Suburban Hospital, I wondered if he would ever play drums on our church's worship team again. His driven, impulsive nature that landed him in the hospital had brought me to the brink of despair many times. As an infant, he would amuse himself by pulling the hair of babies in the nursery or flying through the air on a bicycle off a dock into a dry riverbed, breaking his arm in the process – a consequence he hadn't considered. His mind didn't work like that. Act first – face the consequences later – not maliciously though.

Robert didn't have a malicious bone in his body. He was the kind of child who wept when you stepped on an insect or a worm, a child who wanted to give a home to every stray or wounded animal that crossed his path. I remember when an oriole fell out of its nest and limped its way across our front lawn. Robert was insistent that we try to nurse the bird back to health and wouldn't put the matter to rest until we took it to a wild animal clinic where they promised they would set it free in the wild when the bird was strong enough to survive on its own.

Then there was the day his own bird named Cinderella, a cockatiel we had for several years, died in his hands, apparently from a heart attack which we found out later is common for birds of its species. Fourteen-year-old Robert wept, thinking it was all his fault – giving us a window into the gift of love and tenderness the Lord had bestowed on his character. One day I was so at the end of myself with his behavior that I cried out to God, "Lord! What do you want me to do with this child?"

The Lord answered quickly. "He's a diamond – a diamond in the rough." From that moment on, I saw Robert through a different lens – a diamond in the rough – that the Lord had given us to raise.

While Robert's medical diagnosis was not totally clear, his psychiatrist leaned towards early onset bipolar disorder. The doctors at Suburban Hospital were suspecting this after his first hospitalization where he was diagnosed with severe untreated Attention Deficit Hyperactivity Disorder. It was a difficult diagnosis to make in a child as bipolar disorder is a disease that typically manifests in early adulthood.

Dr. Demitrii Paplos in his book, *The Bipolar Child,* had best described the life our family had been living. He knew that it was no easy task and even made the claim that it was an illness that doctors knew little about and were wary of diagnosing in the first place. He equated living with a child diagnosed with early onset bipolar disorder to a

> war zone, dealing with feelings that alternate from extreme anger at the child, to the most unbelievable yearning to help that child, from rage at the outside world for failing to understand what is happening to them, to exhaustion in trying to deal with the child. And tricked into that welter of truly terrible feelings is shame – shame that one is unable to control his or her own child, and shame at what one begins to put up with and how abnormal one's life has become (Paplos, *The Bipolar Child* (First Edition), p. 242).

Though Robert was still in the process

of being evaluated for this disorder, the symptoms relayed to us by his own physicians and articles we had read on the disease closely described the experiences we had had with Robert even as a young child. His next scheduled doctor's visit had been set to determine whether or not his medication should be changed.

★★★★★

Journal Entry
Robert Hoppel
11/4/00

Lord, please forgive me for all the things I've done that are not of you. Please forgive me for drinking lacquer thinner. Lord, I am a fool ... please have mercy on my soul and show me how to live a life that has constant connection with You. I pray that my meeting with the pastors goes well tomorrow. I'm really unsure as to how I can effectively communicate with You. When I pray, I feel uncomfortable, so I am going to trust that You are listening.

Please help my hospital stay to not be a great setback to some of the things You would have me do. Lord, I want so much to play in the music industry and to be really honest, I am not totally sure if my motives are good or bad. Honest, yes, I must be honest because You know everything.

Lord, I tried to be really focused on other people on Friday and it really made me feel better. Please help me to continue that mindset with everyone. I need the joy of the Lord that I have heard so much about. Sometimes, I just don't feel like being joyful.

I need to stop being upset ... stupid things bother me and I don't think You like that.

CHAPTER 6
TEEN IDOLATRY

Letter to the Editor
Subject: Teen Idolatry

Dear Sir:

I want to let you know how much I appreciated your article in your latest magazine on "Teen Idolatry." We have just been through the most horrendous situation with our 14-year-old son that we feel is directly related to the music he had become interested in. Several times I felt prompted to email for prayer support because his situation was so horrible we kept much of it in confidence to spare him from unnecessary rumors spreading and to spare his family and friends from the devastating details as things unfolded. Our pastor helped us through the worst of it and now that things are in a better place, we are able to open up to trusted people for support. But after reading your article, I wanted to tell you, from firsthand experience, that the effects some of these artists are having on our children is devastating.

Our 14-year-old son, Robert, is a gifted musician and was the drummer on our Church's worship team for two years. He entered public school in sixth grade after having attended private school and/or being homeschooled his entire academic life. He faced many pressures as we know kids do in public school and there were situations that he could and should have handled differently, but he still had his faith and good friends to support him.

He turned 14 the summer before his freshman year of high school and circumstances helped create a downward spiral in his life that we would never have thought possible given the upbringing he had. He started listening to bad music – we don't know how else to label it. He started out just showing an interest, being lured by the musicality of it. He insisted that he wasn't paying attention to the lyrics – that none of this interested him – it was just the music. But the spirit behind the music was so dark and oppressive that I couldn't bear to have it in our house.

We weren't as vigilant as we should have been because he found ways to keep listening to it – downloading MP3 files from the Internet, Napster, and earphones on disc players. We did the best we could as parents to keep him away from the music but the more he listened, the more defiant and addicted he became. His behavior started to transform, acting out in unimaginable ways. In December, he was asked to take a six-month sabbatical from the worship team due to violent outbursts of temper at home.

In January he wanted to leave home and we ended up checking him into a local hospital for evaluation. They ended up attributing a medical cause (Severe Untreated ADHD) to some of the impulsive behavior, but we knew the spiritual dimensions of much of the way he was behaving was due to the music he was listening to. When we finally got a hold of the lyrics of some of the artists, we drew a line in the sand for him. No longer was it a question of bad spirit and bad influence; these lyrics were destroying him and we knew we had to get him away from them. It wasn't easy.

He tried to take his life twice, once with pills, a second time slitting his wrist. We had to call the police twice and the profanity that came out of his mouth while he was being hauled out of our home, double handcuffed – exhausting the strength of six police officers – was unbelievable. They took him to the hospital where he stayed for five days and was diagnosed with major depression. Since he's been home, we've been on a roller coaster of a ride – keeping the music away – something he was able to come to his senses about while away from home. But occasionally a desire will spring up in him and he asks to listen to just one rap – he says he's addicted and that we have no idea how hard it is for him not to be listening to it.

We are keeping it away and while he's not under the influence, his life is starting to turn back to Christ. He's reading his Bible again, back in fellowship with his Christian brothers and sisters, and obeying our rules at home. We're not sure it's over though, because there is still an occasional act of defiance that causes us concern that it's not all out of his system. And school starts again in six weeks and we don't know the influence his peers will have on him again. We hope there has been true repentance in his heart and we hope that he is strong and determined enough to stay away from the music that he himself attributes to the major downswing his life took this past year.

I am writing this to you because we as parents were caught unaware. We had never heard of some of the rap artists my son had been listening to for quite some time. The music itself is very catchy and easy to listen to, but it took awhile before we caught on to the devastating lyrics. It's when you understand the words that the true nature of what's happening is revealed — the lure of the "forbidden fruit" and the devastating consequences when these young listeners "bite" into it.

Robert said one profound thing to us: "Someone ought to write [these artists] and tell them that it's not the way they said it would be." I asked him what he meant by that and he responded, "You know, being hauled off by the police and all — it wasn't very fun." These artists say a lot about what's "fun" — murder, rape, suicide, hatred, rebellion — and it's a battle we've been thrown into on the front lines.

When I read your article, "Teen

Idolatry," I felt impressed to let you know how our family has been touched by this issue. We would covet whatever prayer support you can offer for our son, Robert. We're sure he's not totally out of the woods yet. But I felt that someone should know – perhaps his experience would help some other parents and/or teens be more proactive in the steps they take to keep such a tragedy from happening in their family.

Sincerely,
Jennifer Hoppel

★★★★★

It was three days before I noticed my son's behavior becoming markedly defiant and rebellious. He had been listening to a CD on loan from a friend from school. We had previously trusted our son's judgment in music but suddenly his behavior was spinning out of control. Angry confrontations increased until we stepped in and demanded to listen to the music he had been "glued" to for the past few days. We knew at once that we were in trouble, and we also knew that Robert was in trouble. The effect this music had on him in a short period of time was not unlike a poisonous asp's venom and we hoped and prayed that our intervention had come in time.

I wrote a letter to the editor of a Christian magazine I had been reading, mentioning an article he had written in their latest issue on "Teen Idolatry." This article helped bring some clarity and direction to the issues we had been facing at home. The article highlighted the fact that a lot of the music the kids were listening to was having very bad effects on them, their families, and the culture of the day. He wrote me back affirming our concerns and encouraged Robert to write a letter to some of the artists he had been listening to. He thought perhaps such a letter might help to save some lives of teens caught in the same web of lies and destructive influence that Robert found himself caught up in. He even offered to help publish and distribute such a letter and talk to Robert should Robert ever wish to speak with him.

Robert did not live long enough to write that letter but he did write a song, a rap actually, that documented his own experience with the music he had gotten drawn into and caught up in – the influence of which ultimately brought an end to his life. The name of the particular artist he was addressing in his rap will remain anonymous. The blank could be filled in by many who were popular rap artists of his day.

[ ] EXCLUSIVE
Written by Rob James H.

Chorus Rap

[ ] Exclusive, meet violence patrol, the kids are outta control
[ ] Incorporated, meet violence patrol, the kids are outta control

Verse

Now a days, everybody wanna talk, Like they've got something to say,
But nothing comes out when they flap their lips, just a bunch of gibberish
Yeah, just a bunch of gibberish.
Stop, I'm gonna have to say that that's not right
I've got something for you to make your small night light bright, alright?
You're right, everyone does wanna talk, it's only

a matter of days
Now I'm not everyone but hear me, I do have something to say.
I used to love your dig, man, I thought you had things together
I know now that I'll live to regret that choice forever.
Why did you tell me that drugs and rape are ok?

You lied to me and I believed you and I had to learn the hard way.
A tumble with the cops and a few hospital stays,
Man, it's not dope! It really bites, but you said I'd be alright.
You taught me that anger was the best way to cope
Man you're a fake – so step away from your show.
You influenced my life, I did some pretty crazy things.
Who would have thought [ ] craze was so soon to set in?
You rap about killing, and living the life of a villain
Villain, you're trippin' over your words, and that message is crippling,
And it's choking, and it's bringing great

destruction and it's filling
All the minds of kids just like me, all the minds of kids just like me
Who are foolish enough to think you're the answer, that you were meant to be
And you blame it on your parents 'hey you're the ones that made me.'
Dawg be a man not a boy and take that responsibility
Can you take that responsibility?

Verse

Okay here it is let me ask you one thing,
What will [ ] known to you as [ ] do when he
Reaches judgment day and starts his questioning, before his King,
What will he have to say about all that cussing in his rapping?
Will he say, "Hey! Stop interrogating me, I don't have to take this, I created idolatry!"
Will he deny that with a knife he was cutting morals of the kids?
That he was too blind to see he was influencing?
I wonder what he'll say when he sees he needs God
But it's too late and there's no time to just beg on his knees

Or break down and just ask for that one little chance
To go back but he can't and will he start crying
Or will he get really mad and put his finger up and say
"Sorry I've got news you might find interesting
See I'm [ ] yes I'm the real [ ]
Do you think I'll go to hell with these mortal beings?"
And will God simply sit with a tear in his eye,
And then turn to [ ] and reply his reply:
"For today is the end of [ ]'s reign,
And son sorry say you will see what it means
You will feel the tense pain and the hurt that won't ease.
And you'll see what it means to be eternally
Separated from God, the one you'd not need
Yes, [ ], it's true, why can't you see?
That the one who you denied is Me.
That one who you denied it was Me!"

★★★★★

Journal Entry
Robert Hoppel

Do not be deceived by the lies that have been presented to you.

[ ] has lost all power he has strived to gain and he is not content.

Why do you search for ways to be different? If anything, be different because of what I am doing through you.

★★★★★

Journal Entry
Robert Hoppel

I've been here a long time
I know this place like you know your own
I've been inside my mind
And it's here that I've witnessed al the worst of crimes.

CHAPTER 7
HANSEL AND GRETEL

Untitled
Written by Rob H.

What's this world turnin' out to be?
People livin' on the streets
People denied the right to be free
Artists reaching little kids
Each one taking what he thinks to be his
In the vile name of show biz
Confusing what right and wrong is.

Well, listen to this
I don't care what you think you're doing
I don't care how much dough you're making
I don't care how much you think you're gaining
I don't care how much you think you're hurting

All I see is you hating
And with that hate, you're stating

Like homing missiles, locked on the fans you're feigning
Or should I say brain washing
I'll warn you that Someone is watching
And He is not liking what He is seeing
Villains playing with feelings, cutting the cut that was healing
Slitting the throat that was singing,
Breaking the knees that were kneeling.

'Cause you're showin' kids how to conceal weapons without getting caught
So when they fought, the gun was pulled out, aimed and then shot

Well, that's not how it's supposed to be
Dead bodies washed from sea
To conceal the murder
Thinkin', 'Why did you want to kill me?'

Do you have the answer? No.
Do you know why your best friend is now a foe?
Do you know why there is a body lying on the floor?
Do you know why that suicide note's nailed to the door?

No, I don't think so
I don't think anyone in this fallen world
Is able to know what God knows.

★★★★★

On November 2, 2001, nearly six months after Robert had died, I was driving towards our home on the Dulles Toll Road after dropping off our son, David, at youth group in Reston, Virginia. The traffic in front of me had come to a near complete stop and I had to brake rather quickly to avoid hitting the car in front of us. The next thing I knew, my car had been hit from behind and was being thrown into oncoming traffic coming down the lane to our left. Brakes were screeching, glass was flying, and the sound of crunching metal all around us.

Joshua, who was sitting in the back seat, covered with glass from the rear window that had caved in on top of him, started to cry and asked, "Mommy, what's happening?" The Presence of the Lord filled our car and a peace I've learned to associate with the power of the Holy Spirit overwhelmed me. I looked back at Joshua, looked to the side to see if we were going to be hit again from the cars quickly approaching on our left, and looked up to see the car that had hit us from behind flipping over our car into the lane to the right of us. I said, "Joshua, I don't know, but we are going to be alright. Jesus is here, but we must pray for the people in that car that they won't get hurt!"

The other car landed upside down on the middle of the busy highway in the midst of rush hour traffic. People rushed to our car to see if we were alright. Our car had been totaled and we couldn't move. A kind young man rushed to help us out of the car as gasoline was all over the highway and he was concerned that the car would catch on fire. In the midst of total chaos and confusion, our hearts were kept in perfect peace. We were mostly concerned for the occupants of the car that hit our car, not knowing whether they had lived or died.

When the state trooper arrived, he placed a warm blanket around Joshua as he stood alongside a guardrail on the side of the highway and gave him a trooper teddy bear. Joshua was going to be fine. I asked about the well-being of the other driver who had been extricated from the upside down vehicle and taken to the hospital. The trooper told us that it was a woman and that she had survived the crash and was expected to live. I found out several weeks later that she had been treated and released from the hospital the very next day.

The Lord spoke a word to my heart concerning the accident: "I want you to know in life, and in the midst of evil all around, I'm able to keep you in life." I needed to hear this. I needed to know that in the midst of chaos, confusion, darkness, and despair, God is able to keep us in life. When darkness encroached upon the life of Jesus, He made it clear to all those around Him that what was happening to Him was no accident: "Every day I was with you in the temple courts, and you did not lay a hand on me. But this is your hour—when darkness reigns" (Luke 22:53). God permitted Jesus to be taken to the cross. He was and is in control.

One of the happiest childhood memories I have is being in a play, "Hansel and Gretel," directed by my father at a summer youth center in Ocean Grove, New Jersey. He had directed the stage crew to construct a cardboard "house" and cover it with the biggest cookies I had ever seen in my life.

These were real cookies that we could eat! The final night of the play, the entire cast was invited to descend on the cookie house and eat it all up. It was so much fun!

The story of Hansel and Gretel shines a light on the power of darkness as do most fairy tales that have been passed down through the generations. Hansel and Gretel were drawn to the witch's lair by the sheer delight of feasting on a house made of cookies and candy. They were tired and hungry and the lure of their appetites caused them to throw all caution to the wind. Robert actually wrote a song about it:

Hansel and Gretel
Written by Rob H.

Verse

Innocents, insolence. Two children wanting their own way
Faithfulness, shamefulness will lurk through the night
Deprived and taken by what they thought they loved
Treason, betrayal, don't come through here tonight

Chorus

Cause she is waiting in darkness covered in light
Evil piercing to beckon you, to bring you forth tonight
Cause she will kill you in blackness covered by right
Evil panting to welcome you, to see you through the night

I remember a conversation I had with Robert concerning one of the rap artists who had such a negative influence on his life a year or so prior. He said that when he first listened to it, he physically blushed. He was embarrassed to hear the content of the things his heart and mind were being exposed to. But he said he kept listening to it because the music was good. He was attracted to the quality of musicianship he heard. He said that the more he listened, the more he was drawn in. He said that it was a kind of luring that he just couldn't resist. Eventually, he said, the words didn't bother him. He stopped being embarrassed by it all.

In fact, he started to think it was pretty cool. And then he started reciting it and eventually acting it out.

Mom and Dad,

I'm not good at talking but I have to tell you guys what's on my mind. I don't know what to do. I feel like I'm going crazy because I like rap and you won't let me have it – any rap. I tried to find stuff that was okay and you still said no. But I like rap! And it makes me angry to think that I'm just simply not allowed to have it. And then something like tonight happens and I feel so helpless cause everything I try to do ends up with serious consequences.

I'm sorry about what happened tonight. I'm sorry about what I said tonight. I'm sorry about the fact that rap music can be pretty obscene. My state of anger has turned to helpless and hopeless sorrow. I love you both. I love you two very much but you have to understand that sometimes I just need space. Come to me and tell me that you know that what I'm going through is hard. Tell me that you love me and that you understand. Both of you, please, just come to me.

I did not take anything tonight, I promise you. It makes me a little upset that you keep asking me, but I suppose that's normal given what has happened in the past. I want you two to be a part of me that you never have been before. I want you to love the things I love. I want you to love my cat with all your heart. Dad, please show me you care and just pet her once in a while, both of you, instead of trying to always look out for what's hurting me … show more interest in the things that help. That's all for now (you two think I'm writing a suicide note in here) so I better give this to you now. – Robert

Robert penned this note one evening after we had called the police to come help us bring an episode of rage under control. Nothing happened, we were just scared.

Robert's episodes of violence had the potential to escalate quickly to life-threatening situations. One evening he drank a bottle of champagne which, when mixed with the medicine he was taking for ADHD, sent him into a fit of rage where he started throwing plates out our kitchen window and knives out the plate glass window of our living room.

A man and a woman officer came and went into Robert's room where he had blocked himself off. His room had been trashed. He had taken books, videos, and papers and thrown them all around. We were concerned that he might have taken some pills. After spending a good amount of time with Robert in his room, they came out and asked to speak with us. We told them about the music and that we suspected that this recent episode of rage was triggered because of our insistence to keep rap music out of his hands and out of our home.

The police spoke a very stern word to us, assuring us that we were absolutely right. They said that they had a long talk with Robert and that he was not going to be a danger to us or anyone else. He was just angry, but they told us that they are watching this kind of music destroy a generation of kids – good kids from good homes. They said that we would be shocked to know the behavior they as officers of law and order are having to deal with as a result of the kind of music the kids are being allowed to listen to. They implored us to tow the line in this area – to keep the music away – no matter how angry it made Robert feel. And then they thanked us for calling, told us that our son was a good kid, we were doing a good job and to have a nice day.

Little Things
Written by Rob H.

Did he know? Of course he knew.
What all these things would cause him to do.
Then why did he go on to say, "Why was I so blind of you?"
Did she know? Of course she knew.
What all these things would cause her to do

Then why did she go on to say, "Why was I so blind of you?"
Little boy lies to his mom. Right and wrong just

seem to be gone
Then why did he abandon the truth? "I didn't mean to hurt you."
Little girl hides from her dad cause she's afraid he might be real mad
And why did she abandon her love? "I didn't mean to hurt you."

Chorus

Little kids just brought up to know how to let their bad sides show
Little lies from inside our minds. Little things we can't leave behind.
And I would just like to know why … and I would just like to know why.

CHAPTER 8
BLESSED ARE THOSE WHO MOURN

"Blessed are those who mourn, they will be comforted. ... Blessed are those who are persicuted [sic] because of righteousness, for theirs is the Kingdom of heaven." – Matthew 5:4, 10

I was looking through a trunk we saved of Robert's belongings and came across a spiral notebook that at first glance seemed empty. *Why did I keep it?* I wondered. *Because it was Robert's,* I realized – empty pages or not. I started to flip through the pages to see if he had written anything in it all and to my surprise, in the middle of the notebook, were written those words, unmistakably Robert's writing, spelling and all!

I mentioned it to a friend and she said, "You know, Jenny. That's really odd that he would isolate those verses like that. You know that's not the order they come in Scripture."

I took out my Bible and re-read the Word for myself.

> "Blessed are the poor in spirit
> For theirs is the kingdom of heaven
> Blessed are those who mourn
> For they shall be comforted
> Blessed are the meek
> For they shall inherit the earth
> Blessed are those who hunger and thirst for righteousness
> For they shall be filled
> Blessed are the merciful
> For they shall obtain mercy
> Blessed are the pure in heart
> For they shall see God
> Blessed are the peacemakers
> For they shall be called sons of God
> Blessed are those who are persecuted for righteousness' sake,
> For theirs is the kingdom of heaven.
> Blessed are you when they revile and persecute you,
> And say all kinds of evil against you falsely for My sake.
> Rejoice and be exceedingly glad,

> For great is your reward in heaven,
> for so they
> Persecuted the prophets who were
> before you" (Matthew 5: 3-12).

Then I read the same passage in Luke 5:20-23

> "Blessed are you poor,
> For yours in the kingdom of God.
> Blessed are you who hunger now,
> For you shall be filled.
> Blessed are you who weep now,
> For you shall laugh.
> Blessed are you when men hate you,
> And whey they exclude you,
> And revile you, and cast out your name as evil,
> For the Son of Man's sake.
> Rejoice in that day and leap for joy!
> For indeed your reward is great in heaven,
> For in like manner their fathers did to the prophets."

I checked both accounts of the Beatitudes and found that my friend was right. Nowhere in Scripture do the lines "Blessed are those who mourn" and "Blessed are those who are persecuted" come side by side. Why did Robert choose to write them down like this?

On one of my first visits to Robert's grave, I had a vision. My friend was with me and I related it to her. As I was kneeling down and praying, I saw a vision of Robert being stoned to death. I wondered what this vision meant for no one threw any stones at him – he took his own life. It was one of those moments that I just had to ponder in my heart, not totally understanding it all but sensing that there was significance and I was not to forget the experience.

It wasn't too long after the vision I had at Robert's gravesite that I was reading in Scripture the account of Naboth – the owner of a vineyard who was innocently stoned to death for telling Ahab that he did not want to sell his inheritance – his vineyard – to him.

> And it came to pass after these things that Naboth the Jezreelite had a vineyard which was in Jezreel, next to the palace of Ahab king of Samaria.
>
> So Ahab spoke to Naboth, saying 'Give me your vineyard, that I may

have it for a vegetable garden, because it is near, next to my house; and for it I will give you a vineyard better than it. Or if it seems good to you, I will give you its worth in money.'

But Naboth said to Ahab, 'The Lord forbid that I should give the inheritance of my fathers to you!'

So Ahab went into his house sullen and displeased because of the word which Naboth the Jezreelite had spoken to him; for he had said, 'I will not give you the inheritance of my fathers,' And he lay down on his bed, and turned away his face and would eat no food.

But Jezebel his wife came to him and said to him, 'Why is your spirit so sullen that you eat no food?'

He said to her, 'Because I spoke to Naboth the Jezreelite, and said to him, "Give me your vineyard for money; or else, if it pleases you, I will give you another vineyard for it." And he answered, "I will not give you my vineyard."'

Then Jezebel his wife said to him, 'You now exercise authority over Israel! Arise, eat food, and let your heart be cheerful; I will give you the vineyard of Naboth the Jezreelite.'

And she wrote letters in Ahab's name, sealed them with his seal, and sent the letters to the elders and the nobles who were dwelling in the city with Naboth. She wrote in the letters, saying:

> Proclaim a fast, and seat Naboth with high honor among the people; and seat two men, scoundrels, before him to bear witness against him, saying, "You have blasphemed God and the king." Then take him out, and stone him, that he may die.

So the men of his city, the elders and nobles who were inhabitants of his city, did as Jezebel had sent to them, as it was written in the letters which she had sent to them.

They proclaimed a fast, and seated Naboth with high honor among the people. And two men, scoundrels, came in and sat before him; and the scoundrels witnessed against him, against Naboth, in the presence of the people, saying, 'Naboth has blasphemed God and the king!' Then they took him outside the city and stoned him with stones, so that he died.

Then they sent to Jezebel, saying, 'Naboth has been stoned and is dead.'

And it came to pass, when Jezebel heard that Naboth had been stoned and was dead, that Jezebel said to Ahab, "Arise take possession of the vineyard of Naboth the Jezreelite, which he refused to give you for money; for Naboth is not alive, but dead."

So it was, when Ahab heard that Naboth was dead, that Ahab got up and went down to take possession of the vineyard of Naboth the Jezreelite (1 Kings 21:1-16, NIV).

As I was meditating on this passage of Scripture, I felt as if the Lord gave me insight into how the enemy of our soul works.

We had always felt that Robert's death was linked to spiritual forces of evil at work in his life. This was very evident as he documented the battle in his own journal. Satan *was* trying to kill him and he couldn't get free from the lies that had penetrated his mind, pelting his thoughts like stones or hail. Robert had even written in his journal,

> *"I keep trying to keep Your ways on my mind, but I can't. Satan is trying to lie to me. Please! Tell him to leave me!"*

When I compared Robert's comments with the passage in Scripture concerning Naboth, I saw a pattern of evil behavior:

1. **Naboth was a righteous man.** He had done nothing wrong. He simply had a vineyard someone else wanted and he wouldn't let the other person have it.

2. **Jezebel decided that this wasn't the final word.** There was "authority" in this situation that could be evoked and exercised, regardless of what was right or wrong. Righteousness and the fear of God were never a consideration here.

3. **Jezebel stirred up Ahab**. It's possible that Ahab would have just let it go. Even though he was depressed, he didn't seem so incensed about the situation that he was making any plans to do anything about it. He coveted something that belonged to someone else and was upset that he couldn't have it but it was his wife who took on the offense for him and who knew how to stir things up.

4. **Jezebel was a schemer.** She knew that the king couldn't just go take the vineyard by force so she devised a scheme to get ownership another way. She wrote letters in Ahab's name, putting the authority of the king on it by "sealing them with his seal" and sent them to the elders and nobles of the land.

5. **The elders received the letters in the king's name.** Those letters bore all the weight and authority of the king's seal

so it was as if the king himself was present. It's possible that the king, apart from the influence of his evil wife would have done the right thing and honored Naboth's desire to keep the land for himself. But stirred up by his wicked wife, Jezebel, Ahab allowed the elders to receive false information that not only stirred up the elders to sin against Naboth but also incensed the entire populace of the city where Naboth dwelled. The power behind the lies and the slander was so great that Naboth's good character was distorted before the leaders and the people so much so that they picked up stones and stoned him to death. This is a pattern that can be seen in Scripture over and over again. Oh, the power and destruction of the false report!

I saw this same pattern at work in Robert's life. Scoundrels at work – mostly in his own head – witnessing against him, slandering, criticizing, coveting, inciting – lying against his character – chipping away at his self-esteem – "bothering" him – tormenting – telling him he wasn't worth anything at all and life at its best wasn't worth living. I fasted and prayed for him throughout his ordeal and the Lord kept telling me that he was a "diamond", holy, chosen, and a "special treasure above all the peoples who are on the face of the earth" (Deuteronomy 14:2).

I remember thinking at the time, "Treasure? Lord, it's hard for us to see ourselves as 'treasure!'" Robert's behavior was being influenced by evil and taking its toll among our family and friends but it didn't negate the fact that we, as Christians, including Robert, were God's special treasure. We are a holy people to the Lord, chosen and set apart from the beginning of time to be a people for Himself, sought out and being sanctified to take our place at the marriage supper of the Lamb, whose very blood purchased, redeemed, cleansed and saved us. We are a special treasure indeed, but evil had been moving in to make a second claim like Ahab and Jezebel did in the story of Naboth and his vineyard.

There was a song we used to sing in church in the '70s:

He signed my deed with His atoning blood
He ever lives to make His promise good
Though all the hosts of hell march in to make a second claim
They all march out at the mention of His name
They all march out at the mention of His name.

Ahab tried to make a second claim on Naboth's inheritance. With the help and evil scheming of his wicked wife Jezebel, he succeeded – on earth anyway. The enemy also tried to make a second claim on Robert's inheritance. With the help and scheming of evil driven influences on Robert's life, he succeeded – on earth anyway. When praying about what to put on Robert's gravestone, a very special Scripture came to mind:

> The body is sown in corruption, it is raised in incorruption. It is sown in dishonor, it is raised in glory. It is sown in weakness, it is raised in power. It is sown a natural

body, it is raised a spiritual body (1 Corinthians 15:42-44).

The Lord made something perfectly clear to me shortly after Robert died. The death he died would be no more corrupt, no more dishonorable, and no more weak than the death any one of us is going to die. We all die because of sin. But when "this corruptible has put on incorruption, and this mortal has put on immortality, then shall be brought to pass the saying that is written: 'Death is swallowed up in victory'" (1 Corinthians 15:54).

After reading the account of Naboth in Scripture, I understood why I would have gotten a vision at Robert's gravesite of him being stoned to death. The scoundrels were within – evil thoughts, evil suggestions, evil lies pelting him like stones against the truth that he was a treasure, God's special treasure, chosen, holy, and beloved by the King of Kings.

The Scriptures tell us to take up the helmet of salvation, that we do not wrestle against flesh and blood, but against principalities, against powers, against the rulers of the darkness of this age, and against spiritual hosts of wickedness in the heavenly places (see Ephesians 6:10-18). This is a commandment with a promise. It's interesting that David slew Goliath with a single stone – aimed right at the part of the forehead that his helmet did not protect. Satan knows the areas of weakness in our lives where he can take his aim and throw. He knows our insecurities and vulnerabilities. He knows just what to say, when to say it, and who to say it to and through. He knows how to incite, accuse, manipulate, and persuade. He is a master of deception and lies. He is the ultimate scoundrel and will stop at nothing to make his case against the saints of the Most Holy God.

But we are not without defense against our foe. As we read in Ephesians 6:10-18, we have been given armor to stand against the wiles of the evil one. We have been given the belt of truth, the breastplate of righteousness, the gospel of peace, the shield of faith, the helmet of salvation, and the sword of the Spirit - the truth of God's Word. And we have the Holy Spirit of God who offers refreshment in times of great trial and despair.

CHAPTER 9
THEY SURVIVED

They Survived
By Robert Hoppel

Chorus

And I'll always, always, always be true
And I'll always, always, always love you

Verse

Do you know what it's like
To have to hide
I knew a girl
Who wore a star
She knew what it's like
To live is to survive

★★★★★

Look Back in Time (not finished)
Written by Rob H.

Verse

Go back in time to a child that used to cry out to God
And every day she'd say that prayer hoping someone would hear
But soon her death came upon like a mid-summer storm
And then her prayer for God was fulfilled

Verse

Look back in time to a boy that used to cry himself asleep
For fear his mother now gone had been consumed by that fire
And hear his pure hearted prayer to a God that would hear
But choose to stay for it was all meant to be

Verse

Now search in time for a God that let his only Son die
But not just die, come back again to save us all
For had He not given His life, we would all surely fall

So who are we to say He is cruel or gone
When He is the only one who loves us all

Robert had a difficult time understanding the atrocities of the Holocaust. He had studied it in school, visited the Holocaust Museum in Washington, D.C., and watched the movie *Schindler's List*. The realities of this dark period of world history haunted his mind for weeks. He could not understand how God could have allowed this to happen.

The two songs he wrote about this, "They Survived" and "Look Back In Time," show how God helped Robert reconcile this. The "little girl who wore a star" was the little girl in the movie who eventually was killed. And the chorus to that song represented the voice of Jesus speaking out and saying, "No matter what happens, no matter what evil befalls you or your family, I'll always, always, always be true and I'll always, always, always love you." Robert believed that from the bottom of his heart and he wanted to live to tell others what the Lord had shown him.

One of the pastors Robert used to counsel with had a picture in his office of a man climbing a sheer ice wall. Robert thought that picture was really cool. At the bottom of the picture was a saying, "All things are possible for those who believe." Robert's faith-climb was very much like the man climbing the wall of sheer ice that Robert enjoyed so much. He was a worshiper and the battle for his heart and mind was intense. But even though he faced dangers all around, he believed in and loved God. He wasn't afraid to keep climbing. He just lost his grip and fell.

The night Robert took his life he was tired and cold. He had been playing hard with his friends for three days and had forgotten to take his medicine that the doctors had recently prescribed for him. He was at a point in his medical treatment that the doctors were going to see if his medication could be reduced and Robert really didn't want to take it anyway. He was doing so well and hadn't had a violent episode or mood swing in six months. He was excited that the pastors had invited him back to be the drummer on the church's worship team. Things were going well for him and he had much to look forward to. But the enemy of his soul took advantage of a moment of weakness and moved in like a flood to encourage him to give up and let go.

Shortly after Robert died, I was asked to speak at a weekend retreat and I put together in words the testimony of how the Lord had helped us through the fiery trials we have had to endure, not just concerning Robert, but concerning our son, David, whose life hung in the balance for so many years. After finishing, I took a look at the paper I had written and found myself getting a little upset with God. I told Him, "Lord, I know You are everything You say that You are, but I don't *want* this testimony! This is too much for me – more than I can bear!" And the Lord responded to me in a most unusual way.

My youngest son, Joshua, pulled me over to view a display at the Washington National Zoo one day and insisted that I join him in enjoying a male peacock in full display of his feathers. It was a sight to behold – gorgeous colors, intricate design, and a bold peacock enjoying the full attention of all the spectators who had gathered around to see. I was taken back by the beauty of it all. And then the peacock folded up his feathers and strutted away to the disappointment of those of us who wanted to see more.

I went over to the sign and read that the people who study the habits of male peacocks have come to the conclusion that the male peacock is making a statement while displaying his feathers. He is saying to the world around him that in spite of the weight of these feathers, he is a survivor. His bold display of beauty is in reality his biggest liability, yet fashioned by his Creator's design to defend and allure, not pull down in defeat.

And the Lord spoke to me again, saying, "Your testimony is a heavy weight that you will have to carry behind you the rest of your life. But like the peacock, there will be times when you will be asked to 'display your feathers' and those who see will marvel at the beauty of what I have done in the midst of it all. The weightier the feathers, the more glorious the display."

Look Back in Time
Written by Rob H.

" … *a God that let his only Son die;*
But not just die, come back again to save us all.
For had He not given His life, we would all

surely fall; So who are we to say He is cruel or gone
When He is the only One who loves us all."

They Survived
Written by Rob H.

"I'll always, always, always be true
And I'll always, always, always love you."

CHAPTER 10
THE FATHER'S LOVE

Robert used to have dreams and sometimes he would tell me about them. Most of the time he didn't know what they were about but I thought one dream he relayed to me was profound. I thought I understood it as he recounted to me the details.

Robert and Rebekah, as Robert told me his dream, were walking along the beach together. They were trying to locate the house of an elderly man that Robert had vandalized. Robert had since felt remorseful for his actions and wanted to revisit the place where he had thrown some bottles through the window. He was telling Rebekah that he felt really bad for doing what he had done and wanted to track the elderly gentleman down to apologize.

They came across the run down old cabin on the beach and the elderly gentleman had stepped outside just as they approached. Robert introduced himself as the boy that threw the bottles through his windows and the elderly man kindly smiled and said, "I've been looking for you."

Robert apologized to the man and he said again, "I've been looking all over for you. I want to adopt you!"

Robert remembered feeling very surprised and said to the old man, "Adopt me? I'm the boy that threw the bottles and broke all your windows. Why would you want to adopt me?" By this time they had walked inside the cabin that had since been all cleaned up and the windows replaced, and Robert noticed that the man had framed Robert's birth certificate and hung it on the wall of his cabin.

The old man replied, "I knew that you didn't mean to do it and I've been looking for you. I want you to live with me and I want to be your father and I want you to be my son."

Robert remembered his reaction in his dream of being, as he told me, "totally blown away." And then he heard the sound of glass tinkling in the wind. It was a beautiful sound, making beautiful music, and he followed the sound down a flight of rickety old stairs out to a porch overlooking the sea. He looked up to see some wind chimes that the man had made out of glass – the glass from the broken bottles that Robert had thrown through the windows of the same man's cabin not so very long ago.

And then Robert woke up, not understanding anything but remembering all the details of his dream.

I told Robert that I thought I understood what his dream was all about. I told him that his dream perfectly described the love of God, the Father, who searches for us and longs to be a Father to us, though we've done nothing to deserve His love. And better still, those very acts meant for harm, in Robert's dream represented by the broken bottles thrown through the windows of an innocent old man, God is able to pick up, forgive, and make something beautiful out of it – i.e., the wind chimes made from the broken pieces of the bottles Robert threw through the window. Robert expected judgment from the old man, but instead he received mercy, love, and grace.

I further told Robert that I thought this dream was from God to encourage him that his life was not beyond repair and furthermore that God was going to take the years of brokenness and make something beautiful out of it. I think this encouraged Robert and as I reflect on that dream today, I still believe it's true that God can take what seems to be an irreversible act of despair and make something beautiful from it. I have already heard the music of "wind chimes" from broken parts of Robert's life and testimony.

Most of Robert's friends have wholeheartedly dedicated their life paths to serving and following the Lord Jesus Christ, one committing his life to becoming a youth pastor to help teens like Robert sort through the tangled emotions of adolescent despair. Others became worship leaders and pastors, and his brother David is now a hospice chaplain, passionate to help families and friends of loved ones going through the same process of grief that he himself endured after losing his older brother in such a sudden and violent way. Robert is home with his Father in heaven but his life lives on in the hearts of those he sowed so passionately into, though broken and confused and unable to overcome the darkness that had clouded his mind and weakened his heart and resolve.

Robert, the day you took your life was rainy and gloomy. We wish you had lived to see the day that followed. The sky was blue and the sun was shining as we gathered around in a circle, holding hands, to pray for your safe return. The sun was shining the day you took your life, too, but you couldn't see it behind the clouds. God, like the sun, is always there, no matter what lies between. He is always there to replenish and redeem. And though your absence has brought new clouds to our life here on earth, we look forward to the music we know we will hear one day from the windchimes the Lord has already made – a beautiful composition from the Creator who knew you, formed you, and brought you from our home to His ... from angels' holy hands.

AFTERWORD

Shortly after Robert died, my husband, Steve, and I got involved with prison ministry through Outward Focused International, serving the inmate population in Pennsylvania State Correctional facilities. Our team supported the ministry's founder, Jim Newsom, by doing workshops with the incarcerated men, sharing our stories and testimonies about how God can still work in our lives in the midst of challenging and difficult circumstances. For the most part, the workshops focused on trials and redemption, and the grace and favor of a loving and merciful God.

The last workshop we would conduct focused on fruitful suffering, using the story of Naomi and Ruth to show how God worked through a family crisis (the loss of husbands and sons) and rewrote the narrative of these suffering ladies' stories to bring great redemption and hope to their futures.

Had Naomi and Ruth not suffered such great loss and responded as they did, they would not have been mentioned in the generational story of our Lord and Savior, Jesus Christ.

Many of the men incarcerated in those facilities had suffered great loss. One inmate had lost his two-year-old son in a drowning incident and the sorrow and grief he experienced changed his behavior. It made him "crazy," and he ended up in prison for an infraction that he most probably would not have committed had this tragedy not occurred. Another inmate was a former firefighter who told me that on one of his calls he had to watch a family burn alive in a car wreck that neither he nor his fellow firefighters were able to save. His character changed after that incident, and he too ended up in prison as a result of bad choices he made that he definitely would not have made otherwise.

The hope we tried to bring through our many workshops was that great loss does not have to lead to great tragedy. God can redeem anyone's story, like He did with Joseph in the Bible and Naomi and Ruth. We do not have to allow the loss of life dictate our behavior; that loss doesn't have to be the final word. God always has the final word and confident of this, we can look to the future with hopeful anticipation for the fruit our sufferings will bear. Romans 8:28 says that "All things work together for good for those who love God and are called according to His Purposes." All means all - hardships and tragedies included.

In addition to prison ministry, I have spent the last 15 years working in the public school system in Montgomery County, Maryland. That was a call I sensed in 2009 after trying to help our son, David, navigate the difficulties and challenges in public education as a special needs child. My time serving there has been fruitful and productive, and I thank God daily for the opportunities I have to make a difference where and when I can. Nothing has been wasted. And God's Word to us through the years has carried us through the trials and has proven to be steadfast, faithful, and true, as He promised in His Word:

> "But for you who revere my name, the Sun of Righteousness will rise with healing in its wings. And you will go out and leap like calves

released from the stall . . ." (Malachi 4:1).

"Fear not, for I have redeemed you; I have called you by your name, you are Mine. When you pass through the waters, I will be with you; and through the rivers, they shall not overflow you. When you walk through the fire, you shall not be burned, nor shall the flame scorch you. For I am the Lord your God, the Holy One of Israel, your Savior" (Isaiah 43:1-3).

www.ingramcontent.com/pod-product-compliance
Lightning Source LLC
LaVergne TN
LVHW051524070426
835507LV00023B/3280